HEALTH

Andrew J. Milson, Ph.D.
Content Consultant
University of Texas at Arlington

Acknowledgments

Grateful acknowledgment is given to the authors, artists, photographers, museums, publishers, and agents for permission to reprint copyrighted material. Every effort has been made to secure the appropriate permission. If any omissions have been made or if corrections are required, please contact the Publisher.

Instructional Consultant: Christopher Johnson, Evanston, Illinois

Teacher Reviewers: Heather Rountree, Bedford Elementary School, Bedford, Texas

Photographic Credits
Front Cover, Inside Front Cover, Title Page ©Tim Gainey/Alamy. **4** (bg) ©Danita Delimont/Gallo Images/Getty Images. **6** (bg) ©Thomas Coex/AFP/Getty Images. **8** (bg) Mapping Specialists. **10** (bg) ©Marco Baroncini/Corbis. **11** (bl) ©Sebastian Kaulitzki/Alamy. **13** (bg) ©Luis M. Tello Pérez/teseum/Flickr. **14** (bg) ©Andrew Caballero-Reynolds/Getty Images. **16** (bg) ©David R. Frazier Photolibrary, Inc./Alamy. **17** (tl) ©Thomas Stankiewicz/LOOK Die Bildagentur der Fotografen GmbH/Alamy. **19** (bg) ©Bruno Morandi/Hemis/Corbis. (bc) Mapping Specialists. **20** (bg) ©Herbert Scholpp/Westend61GmbH/Alamy. **22** (bg) ©Feliciano dos Santos. **23** (tl) ©Feliciano dos Santos. **24** (br) ©Feliciano dos Santos. **25** (bg) ©Feliciano dos Santos. **27** (t) ©St Petersburg Times/James Borchuck/The Image Works. **28** (tr) ©jo unruh/istockphoto. **30** (tr) ©Bruno Morandi/Hemis/Corbis. (br) ©jo unruh/istockphoto. **31** (tr) ©Luis M. Tello Pérez /teseum/Flickr. (bg) ©Duncan Smith/Photodisc/Getty Images. (br) ©Jake Lyell/Alamy. (bl) ©Alamy Creativity/Alamy.

MetaMetrics® and the MetaMetrics logo and tagline are trademarks of MetaMetrics, Inc., and are registered in the United States and abroad. The trademarks and names of other companies and products mentioned herein are the property of their respective owners. Copyright © 2010 MetaMetrics, Inc. All rights reserved.

Pictures of HEALTH

A family in Mongolia shares a meal at home. With an average life expectancy of around 68 years, children born in Mongolia have a good chance of knowing their grandchildren.

WHAT FACTORS AFFECT LIFE EXPECTANCY AROUND THE WORLD?

It's midnight in France and in the Congo. At the same moment in both places, a baby is born. Thousands of miles apart, each new mother holds her infant in her arms and wishes him a long and healthy life.

But will their wishes come true? Not necessarily. Chances are good that the child born in France will live long enough to meet his grandchildren and maybe his great-grandchildren. The child born in the Congo, though, may not live to adulthood.

WHO WILL LIVE? FOR HOW LONG?

Health is an important human concern. We all want to be healthy regardless of who we are or where we live.

One way of looking at health is through **life expectancy**, or the average number of years a person can expect to live. Not everyone has the same life expectancy. A person born in Spain, for instance, has an average life expectancy of 81 years. In Nigeria, though, life expectancy is just 52.

Why do these inequalities exist? Why are the prospects for a long and healthy life so different around the world?

In this book, you'll read about some factors that influence life expectancy. Health is about more than just lifestyle and **heredity**, which is the passing of genes down through generations. It isn't even only a medical issue. Health is a reflection of society, including culture, politics, economics, and access to **health care**—that is, medical services.

This laboratory in France makes a medicine to prevent H1N1, a severe type of flu that can spread very quickly. Medicines such as these are expensive to manufacture and distribute and can be slow to reach remote or rural areas of developing countries.

OUTBREAKS AND BREAKTHROUGHS

Health has become a global issue. Diseases don't recognize borders. A **virus** is a tiny organism that infects living cells with disease. One of these can erupt in Malawi on Monday and can be in New York or Tokyo by Tuesday.

Scientific discoveries cross borders too. Sometimes it takes a team to solve a medical problem—including experts from around the world who combine knowledge and resources.

Scientists still don't understand many of the factors that affect life expectancy. For example, what explains the clusters of seniors around the world who live active lives into their 90s? How do they stay so healthy for so long?

There are no simple solutions to health problems around the world. For example, wealth does not always guarantee good health. One measure of a country's wealth is **GDP per capita**, or the value of the goods a country produces per person. However, GDP per capita is not necessarily linked to life expectancy. Other factors may be more important to good health, such as a balanced diet, regular exercise, and being part of a strong community.

The good news is that we can advance good health everywhere on Earth. Two countries that are confronting health issues are Burkina Faso, in Africa, and Sardinia, which is in Europe. Both countries show that positive steps can be taken toward improving health.

LIFE EXPECTANCY AND INCOME

	LIFE EXPECTANCY	GDP PER CAPITA	LEADING CAUSE OF DEATH OR ILLNESS
Japan	84 years	$34,000	Stroke
France	81 years	$35,000	Cancer
United States	78 years	$48,100	Coronary heart disease
Mexico	77 years	$15,100	Coronary heart disease
Brazil	73 years	$11,600	Coronary heart disease/stroke
India	67 years	$3,700	Coronary heart disease
Russia	66 years	$15,700	Coronary heart disease
Kenya	63 years	$1,700	HIV/AIDS

Sources: *CIA World Factbook*; World Health Organization, 2012

Explore the Issue

1. **Summarize** In what ways is health a global issue?

2. **Compare and Contrast** How does life expectancy in countries with a high GDP per capita compare with life expectancy in countries with a low GDP per capita?

Health Concerns

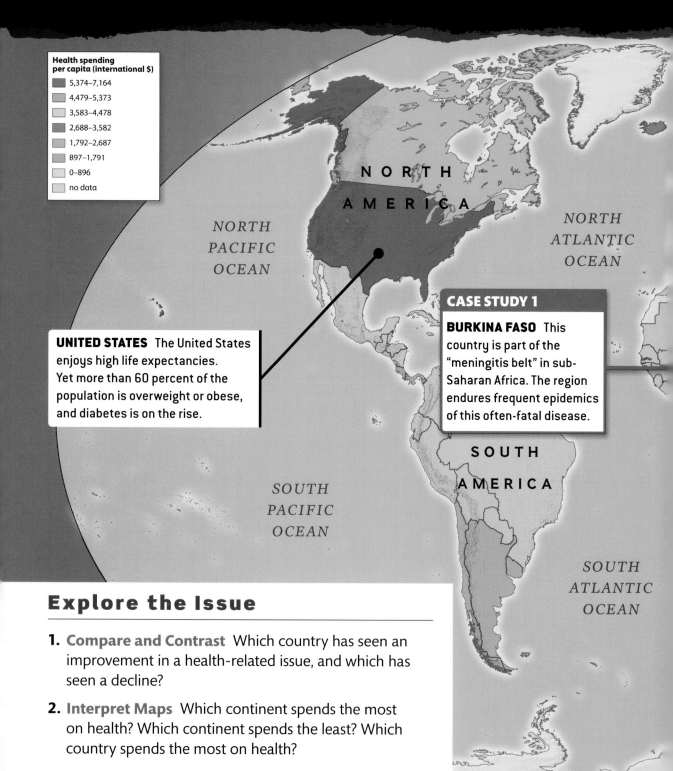

Health spending per capita (international $)

- 5,374–7,164
- 4,479–5,373
- 3,583–4,478
- 2,688–3,582
- 1,792–2,687
- 897–1,791
- 0–896
- no data

NORTH AMERICA

NORTH PACIFIC OCEAN

NORTH ATLANTIC OCEAN

UNITED STATES The United States enjoys high life expectancies. Yet more than 60 percent of the population is overweight or obese, and diabetes is on the rise.

CASE STUDY 1

BURKINA FASO This country is part of the "meningitis belt" in sub-Saharan Africa. The region endures frequent epidemics of this often-fatal disease.

SOUTH AMERICA

SOUTH PACIFIC OCEAN

SOUTH ATLANTIC OCEAN

Explore the Issue

1. **Compare and Contrast** Which country has seen an improvement in a health-related issue, and which has seen a decline?

2. **Interpret Maps** Which continent spends the most on health? Which continent spends the least? Which country spends the most on health?

ARCTIC OCEAN

EUROPE

ASIA

AFRICA

NORTH
PACIFIC
OCEAN

RUSSIA Russia's health care system has experienced declines in recent years. As a result, Russia is one of the few countries where life expectancy has dropped.

INDIA Infectious disease was once the main health concern in India. Now, however, changes in the Indian diet and lifestyle have made heart disease the leading cause of death.

CASE STUDY 2

SARDINIA In certain mountain regions on the island of Sardinia, the rate at which men live to be 100 years old is 10 times the rate in the United States. Women live longer, too, though the global comparison is less dramatic than for men.

PHILIPPINES Infant mortality rates here have improved. The rate decreased from 42 deaths per 1,000 live births in 1990 to 23 deaths per 1,000 live births in 2010.

INDIAN
OCEAN

AUSTRALIA

N
W E
S

| 0 | 1,000 | 2,000 Miles |

| 0 | 1,000 | 2,000 Kilometers |

ANTARCTICA

Meningitis EPIDEMIC in Burkina Faso

A mother awaits treatment for her sick child in a hospital in sub-Saharan Africa.

OUTBREAK!

It starts as a sudden, fierce headache and fever with nausea. Without treatment, up to 50 percent of its victims die, some in a single day. Even those who survive may suffer hearing loss or brain damage. Children are the most vulnerable.

"It" is meningitis (men-in-JY-tis), and from December to June—Africa's dry season—the disease spreads rapidly through the northern part of sub-Saharan Africa. This group of countries, which extends from Senegal to Ethiopia and includes Burkina Faso, is called the "meningitis belt."

Meningitis is caused by bacteria that attack the lining surrounding the brain and spinal cord. When the cold temperatures and dusty winds of Africa's dry season irritate the nose and lungs, the bacteria can spread more easily through coughing, sneezing, sharing food, and close contact. Overcrowded housing increases the risk of spreading germs. Once a meningitis outbreak begins in this region of 450 million, it's not long before an epidemic is underway.

KEEPING A GLOBAL VILLAGE WELL

Epidemics, or the rapid spread of infectious diseases among many people, are as old as humanity. An epidemic becomes a **pandemic** when a disease crosses borders and spreads around the world.

Meningococcus bacteria is the cause of meningitis.

Ease of international travel today means "the whole world is now one village," says Nathan Wolfe, a National Geographic Emerging Explorer and **epidemiologist** (ep-i-dee-mee-AH-loh-jist), or person who studies epidemics. Wolfe and other scientists are working to find ways of detecting and stopping epidemics early, before they become pandemics.

Although meningitis occurs all over the world, its impact in sub-Saharan Africa is harsher because so many people there are poor. In a region with few doctors, little money for medicine, and no easy way to treat the sick, illness spreads easily. In sub-Saharan Africa, those with the greatest need for health care have the fewest resources for helping themselves.

STOPPING A KILLER

Epidemics can be stopped, and science and medicine are working to determine how.

Once an epidemic has begun, it's almost too late to fight back. The best way to beat an epidemic is to keep it from starting. **Vaccines**, or substances that protect a person from an illness, are important tools in battling epidemics. At one time, the World Health Organization (WHO) estimated that vaccines prevented up to 70 percent of the expected cases of meningitis.

Still, it wasn't enough. Even with vaccines, thousands in Africa became sick and died each year because the existing vaccines weren't effective enough. They could not be given to young children. They also wore off quickly, requiring millions to be revaccinated every year.

The answer was a better vaccine. Yet finding one seemed almost impossible. The type of meningitis common in Africa—meningitis A—is unfamiliar in the rest of the world, which means vaccines available elsewhere wouldn't help. A new vaccine, specific to Africa, had to be created. But who would do it? Developing and bringing a new vaccine to market can cost up to $500 million.

IT TAKES A VILLAGE TO SAVE A VILLAGE

It took a special partnership, spanning four continents and lasting nearly a decade, to meet the challenge. In 2001, a dedicated global effort called the Meningitis Vaccine Project began. It brought together private foundations, the World Health Organization, the U.S. Centers for Disease Control and Prevention, the U.S. Food and Drug Administration, and a company in India in a unique collaboration. Their goal was to find a new meningitis A vaccine that offered greater protection but was still affordable.

The clock was ticking. The 2009 meningitis epidemic was devastating, infecting more than 88,000 people and killing more than 5,000. This killer was still on the loose. The team not only had to develop the vaccine, but also had to figure out a way to get it to the children in Africa who needed it most.

A health worker from Doctors Without Borders administers vaccines to children in sub-Saharan Africa. Organizations such as these deliver life-saving vaccines in poor or remote areas.

Health workers set up equipment to begin a vaccine campaign in sub-Saharan Africa.

RESULTS IN RECORD TIME

The solution, however, was close at hand. By the start of the dry season in December 2010, the new vaccine was ready. Named MenAfriVac, the medicine was everything the Meningitis Project team hoped for. It was specific to Africa's form of meningitis. It could be given to children as young as one year old and offered disease protection lasting several years, which is important in ending annual epidemics.

The vaccine had taken nearly ten years to develop. Still, the team was pleased. Ten years was record time. Delays of up to 20 years for a new vaccine are not unusual for Africa. The team had found a way to produce the new vaccine for less than 50 cents per dose.

Burkina Faso was selected as the first country to try MenAfriVac on a large scale. Home to nearly 14 million people in West Africa, Burkina Faso had been particularly hard hit by meningitis early in 2010. More than 600 people had died.

THE END OF A PLAGUE

As the dry season began late in 2010, health care workers rolled out a huge vaccination campaign in Burkina Faso. Hundreds of volunteers were recruited and trained. Some travelled long distances to deliver the vaccine in rural areas. The vaccine itself had to be handled carefully so it would not lose effectiveness.

Six months after Burkina Faso received the vaccine, officials reported just four confirmed cases of meningitis—compared to more than 4,000 cases the season before! A disease that has plagued Africa for 100 years may finally be under control, thanks to the efforts of those who developed the vaccine.

Explore the Issue

1. **Find Main Idea and Details** What health problem tends to occur each year in Africa during the dry season? What makes this problem so serious?

2. **Identify Problems and Solutions** How have economic conditions in the region contributed to the problem?

Sheep farmers herd their flock on the island of Sardinia. The rural lifestyle here includes plenty of exercise.

A LONG LIFE IN Sardin

AN ANCIENT LAND

Rough and rocky, the island of Sardinia rises out of the dark blue ocean about 150 miles from the western coast of Italy. The second largest island in the Mediterranean after Sicily, Sardinia is also one of the most ancient. Geologists estimate that Sardinia was formed about 570 million years ago when continents were still taking shape and the seas were warm and shallow. Sardinia makes dinosaurs seem young!

Strong families, such as the one shown here, are one factor in longevity in Sardinia.

So, old is nothing new here. The barren mountain slopes are much as they were when the Romans, Greeks, and Phoenicians conquered Sardinia thousands of years ago. Sheep and goats still graze the steep pastures as they have for centuries.

As one of Italy's most ancient regions, Sardinia is used to sticking with traditions. The ancient Romans reportedly considered Sardinia "the most worthless of provinces." However, the **longevity**, or long life span, of the people of Sardinia suggests they are doing something right.

THE OLD MEN OF THE MOUNTAINS

Suddenly, old is "hot" here, as in something that everyone wants to copy. Sardinia turns out to be an outstanding environment for people living exceptionally long, vigorous lives.

The world's highest concentration of male **centenarians**—people who are 100 or more years old—lives in the central mountains of Sardinia. And these seniors aren't just still alive; they're also fit. It's not unusual for 103-year-olds to arm-wrestle, tend sheep, ride bikes, and hike the mountains. Cancer and heart disease are relatively rare.

In 2002, 5 of the world's 40 oldest people lived in Sardinia. Out of Sardinia's total population of 1.6 million, 220 people were at least 100 years old—twice the world average. How do they do it?

INSIDE THE BLUE ZONES

There is a name for places like Sardinia: "Blue Zones." The name comes from the colored pen a researcher used to mark a map of Sardinia when he wanted to indicate where an abundance of healthy seniors lived. Since then, the term has come to apply to any community with exceptional life expectancy.

In 2004, with support from the National Geographic Society and the National Institute of Aging, researchers set out to identify and study Blue Zones for their secrets to longevity. They identified Blue Zones worldwide for their research.

Sardinia, Italy Men in the mountainous central region here reach age 100 at a rate 10 times that of men in the United States.

Okinawa, Japan Average life expectancy is 84 years, making it one of the highest in the world.

Nicoya, Costa Rica People here spend a fraction of what the United States invests in health care, yet they enjoy longer and healthier lives.

Loma Linda, California Members of a Seventh Day Adventist group here—a faith that emphasizes healthy living—lead the United States in life expectancy.

WHAT THE DANISH TWINS TOLD US

The first thing to note is what researchers did not find. In 1996 Danish scientists published a study that compared the cause of death of more than 2,800 sets of identical twins. The study suggests that heredity plays a far smaller role in determining life span than scientists once thought. Inherited characteristics account for only about 25 percent of someone's health and length of life. Lifestyle accounts for the remaining 75 percent.

If those percentages are correct, then your life span has less to do with who your relatives are than with who your friends and neighbors are and what you do together. In other words, cultural and environmental factors are important elements of longevity.

Yet the various Blue Zones are very diverse, culturally and geographically. They range from the lush tropics of Costa Rica to the parched hills of Sardinia. What could these places possibly have in common?

The elderly in Sardinia, such as these women on their way to a religious procession, typically enjoy good health well into their 80s and 90s.

BLUE ZONES AROUND THE WORLD

Loma Linda, California

Sardinia, Italy

Okinawa, Japan

Nicoya, Costa Rica

Fresh fruits and vegetables sold in markets such as this one are a part of the healthy eating habits of the people of Sardinia.

SURPRISING FINDINGS ABOUT DIET

As it turns out, they have a lot in common—but not necessarily factors that were thought to be related to longevity. One common factor is exercise. In the Blue Zones, people lead lives of constant physical activity. They walk everywhere, run up and down stairs, and do their own yard work. Most tend gardens. What they don't do is work out. They just work. And because they have few labor-saving devices, such as dishwashers and electric hedge trimmers, they work hard.

Also Blue Zone inhabitants don't follow a strict diet. Yet one thing the Blue Zones share is the habit of eating more plant-based foods than meat. Meals include lots of vegetables and **legumes**, a plant family that includes peas, beans, lentils, and peanuts. Food is served in ways that discourage overeating.

FAMILY AND COMMUNITY

The real secret to longevity, though, seems to lie in how society is organized. In the Blue Zones, communities have a sense of family. Adult children watch out for aging parents, and aging parents watch out for the grandchildren. Family is a priority, as are friends.

Inhabitants of the Blue Zones also tend to share religious beliefs. People meet regularly to attend services. Customs such as these bring about a strong sense of community. People are not isolated, which is especially important for good health among the elderly.

Finally, people in the Blue Zones possess a sense of purpose. Some care for family. Others teach a skill or share knowledge. People in Blue Zones know why they are getting up every morning, and this purpose provides a reason for life—a life that is long and healthy.

Explore the Issue

1. **Describe Geographic Information** Where is Sardinia located and what is the terrain like in the Blue Zone on the island?

2. **Form and Support Opinions** Do you think that any community could improve life expectancy by adopting qualities of a Blue Zone? Why or why not?

Feliciano dos Santos

Sings Songs of Wellness

Santos, on the left, performs songs about washing hands, boiling water, and preventing disease, but he sings them in tribal languages to help get his message across.

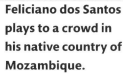

THE GUITAR MAN

In a tiny community in southeast Africa, a world-renowned musician and his band tune their guitars. As a crowd gathers, the band begins to play, everyone swaying to the beat. Are they singing songs about romance, fame, or getting rich? Not exactly:

> *Let's wash our hands*
> *Let's wash our hands*
> *For the children to stay healthy*
> *For the uncles to stay healthy*
> *For the mothers to stay healthy*
> *We build latrines*
>
> —Feliciano dos Santos

Feliciano dos Santos plays to a crowd in his native country of Mozambique.

This musician is more than a rock star. His name is Feliciano dos Santos, and he is a National Geographic Emerging Explorer on a mission to advance the health of Mozambique's poor.

Santos uses music to teach people how to combat disease carried by contaminated water. His lyrics speak of simple things, such as washing hands. Yet his vision is far-reaching. Santos believes he can advance his homeland's economic development by improving **sanitation**, the removal of trash and sewage to prevent disease. He is saving lives with songs.

EMERGING FROM POVERTY TO HOPE

National Geographic's Emerging Explorers Program supports the efforts of gifted young people who have the potential and the commitment to improve the world. As an Emerging Explorer, Santos has focused his improvement efforts on a part of northern Mozambique called Niassa. This area is one of the poorest places on Earth—and it is where Santos was born and raised. More than 60 percent of Niassa's population is **illiterate**, meaning they cannot read or write. Few homes have running water. The average life expectancy is 42 years.

The World Health Organization estimates that unclean water and unsanitary conditions cause 80 percent of illness worldwide. As a child in Niassa, Santos contracted polio from contaminated water. Polio is a highly contagious disease that can cause paralysis and even death. The disease left Santos partially disabled and determined to protect others in Niassa.

THE POWER OF MUSIC TO HEAL

In 1977, a civil war broke out in Mozambique. It claimed close to a million lives and devastated the country's economy. In the aftermath, Santos was determined to help his homeland recover. He started a band called Massukos, which means "nourishing fruit." Music, he believed, would address the psychological scars the war had left on the people of Mozambique. The music of Massukos builds on the melodies, rhythms, and dialects of Niassa.

In time, Santos and his band became famous throughout Africa and even overseas. Yet Santos kept returning to Niassa, committed to helping the people in his homeland despite the challenges. The region remains deeply impoverished.

SONGS AND SANITATION

In 2000, Santos founded a nonprofit organization called Estamos. The mission of Estamos is to provide clean water throughout Niassa by installing water pumps and low-cost, sustainable sanitation facilities.

The project is succeeding. Villagers have installed thousands of "EcoSan" portable bathrooms. These facilities are brick-lined to keep bacteria from infiltrating the groundwater supply. After six months of composting, the contents become fertilizer that farmers use in their fields. Niassa now has a basic sanitation system.

In addition, Santos is using music to teach people better **hygiene**, or the practice of keeping clean to prevent disease. One of Massukos's greatest hits is called "Tissambe Manja," or "Wash Our Hands." "Clean water is a basic human right, yet so many don't have it," says Santos. "I'm using my music to be the voice of people who have no voice."

Santos speaks to children about clean water.

Explore the Issue

1. **Analyze Causes** What are some of the factors contributing to Mozambique's low life expectancy?

2. **Identify Problems and Solutions** Why is Santos successful at teaching people about good health practices?

"I'm using my music to be the voice of people who have no voice." —Feliciano dos Santos

Santos writes songs in traditional melodies so people can remember the message even when the music is over.

Put On a Health Fair

A health fair is an event that includes displays and demonstrations about good health habits. You will be taking part in a health fair in your classroom or school that will raise awareness of healthful practices. Who knows? You might add years to people's lives—and life to their years!

IDENTIFY

- Find out what some of the health issues are in your community. Ask friends, family, and neighbors what they think are the important aspects of daily life that keep them healthy.

- Identify the gaps. What things do you think people need to do to improve their health?

- With three or four classmates, research and plan to take part in a health fair in your classroom or school.

RESEARCH

- For the health fair, your group will have a booth to present information about a specific healthful practice, such as exercising regularly.

- Begin by deciding what healthful practice to present. Another example might be to show people how to shop for and prepare a healthful meal.

- Use library resources or the Internet to research your topic.

Students in Florida do jumping jacks as part of an exercise campaign.

ORGANIZE

- Plan how you will create your booth and present your information in an interesting way.

- Create a visual display that shows the healthful practice. The display could be a poster, or you could even use presentation software.

- Include a demonstration. For example, one member of your group could demonstrate simple ways to build exercise into daily life.

SHARE

- On the day of the health fair, set up your booth and prepare for your demonstration.

- As visitors come to your booth, greet them politely, show them your visual display, and present your demonstration.

- Ask visitors whether they have any questions and provide thorough answers.

- Take photos or make a video as a record of your presentation.

WRITE

Write a TV News Story

Discoveries that improve human health are happening all the time. Some involve complicated technology. However, many others don't. Some of the most important breakthroughs in health have come from using everyday things in new ways. What are some of these discoveries? Why are they effective? Your assignment is to research and write a script for a TV news story that informs your audience about one low-cost, high-impact discovery that is improving people's health care.

RESEARCH

Use the Internet, books, and articles to research and answer the following questions:

- Why is this discovery important? Use facts to explain who's affected by it and how.
- How is this discovery similar to or different from other discoveries in this field? What makes it unique and newsworthy?
- Who are the experts in this field and what do they think?

DRAFT

Review your notes and write a first draft of the script.

- Start with a statement that introduces your topic clearly and previews what is to follow. Explain why you're reporting about the story from your location. Consider sharing an anecdote or presenting a dramatic fact to illustrate the discovery and engage the listener.
- The body of your script should use relevant facts, definitions, concrete details, quotations, and other information and examples. In addition, use interviews to explain why this discovery matters.
- The conclusion should follow from and support the information presented in the body of the script. Explain how this discovery could affect the listener and why it matters.

REVISE & EDIT

Read your script aloud to make sure it's interesting and clear.

- Does the introduction clearly identify the discovery? Does it capture the listener's attention?
- Does the body of the script include facts to inform your audience about the discovery and its potential?
- Does the script end with a logical conclusion based on the facts and interviews?
- What idea will your listeners take away from the news story? Be sure that this is the most important idea.

Be sure to recheck all your facts and the spelling of all the words in your script to ensure accuracy.

PUBLISH & PRESENT

Practice delivering your script as if you were a TV news reporter. What visuals or interviews would you include? Then record yourself. Ask for permission to "air" your news story by emailing it to family and friends or by sharing it through your school's media center.

Visual GLOSSARY

centenarian *n.*, a person who is 100 or more years old

epidemic *n.*, the rapid spread of an infectious disease among many people

epidemiologist *n.*, a person who studies epidemics

GDP per capita *n.*, an estimation of the value of goods produced by each person in a country

health care *n.*, medical services

heredity *n.*, the passing of genes from one generation to the next

hygiene *n.*, the practice of keeping clean to prevent disease

illiterate *adj.*, unable to read or write

legume *n.*, a plant family that includes peas, beans, lentils, and peanuts

life expectancy *n.*, the average number of years a person can expect to live

longevity *n.*, a long life span

pandemic *n.*, an epidemic that has spread around the world

sanitation *n.*, the removal of trash and sewage to prevent disease

vaccine *n.*, a substance that protects a person from an illness

virus *n.*, a tiny organism that infects living cells with disease

centenarian

hygiene

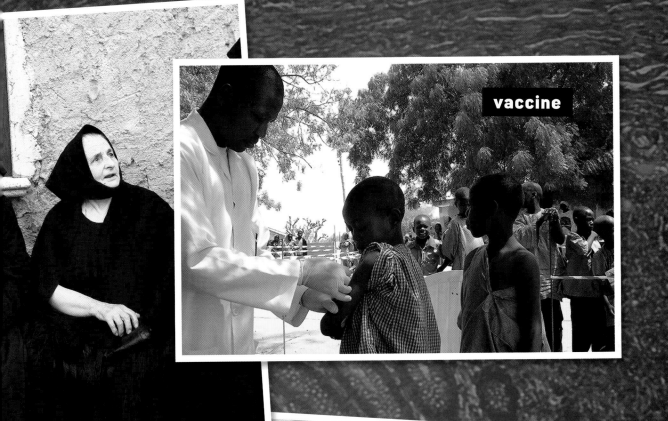

vaccine

legume

health care

INDEX

SKILLS